Lord, My Lord

By Jaye Murphy

PublishAmerica
Baltimore

PublishAmerica has allowed this work to remain exactly as the author intended, verbatim, without editorial input.

Hardcover 978-1-4512-9998-4
Softcover 978-1-4489-3900-8
PUBLISHED BY PUBLISHAMERICA, LLLP
www.publishamerica.com
Baltimore

Printed in the United States of America

I want to dedicate this book to my husband whose love and encouragement kept me going a lot of times when I would often question my calling. He prayed for me in my weary moments when I couldn't or wouldn't pray for myself. Also, I 'd like this, my first published book, to be dedicated to my parents who have always embraced me with their love through some very hard times in my life, as I know that God has kept me through many of their prayers.

INTRODUCTION

Most of what I write is a small piece of me or an association to my life that God has inspired me to share. He is my utmost inspiration, and as such, he has inspired me to share my personal life situations, my frustrations, my strongholds, my prayers, and my struggles as a Christian—ultimately taking it all and using it as my ministry. This compilation of poems that I share with you are from a place that I would normally keep closed off. That is why I know it is God prompting me to share. Perhaps, there is someone out there who may read a poem and say "that's how I feel" or "that's what I'm going through", or perhaps "look how God moved in her life". I share such personal aspects of myself to show you all that you are not alone in your Christian struggle. I am also hoping that one would read my poems from beginning to end and notice the evolution of me throughout—how I came from a place of such unknowing and uncertainty and ended in a place surrounded by God's love, grace, mercy and spiritual wisdom upon my life. It is my desire that you pull something for yourself from many of the poems and be blessed by them. God bless. ☻

(note: All bold print represents the voice of the Holy Spirit.)

INNER PEACE (SEARCHING)

I always seem to get myself in tight situations...
That strain my life, my heart and mind, and cause complications
I need to take time and self heal before I self destruct
I need to find a path in my life that doesn't hurt as much
I need to find a road to joy and inner peace
Instead of traveling down the path of pain, anger, and grief
Soul searching, heart healing—that's what I need
Peace of mind, a rested soul, I need to find for me

THE TEMPLE

So young and unknowing
So inexperienced
So unprepared and unaware
Of the irrefutable damage

Yet determined to have
Her sensationalized idea of love
Ready to give such a large part of herself
Not truly knowing all it consists of

She needs to prove herself to him
It's just that simple
Never really understanding
Her body is a temple

She engages herself
After all, she was now his "girlfriend"
Now feeling uncomfortable, distasteful
And ready for it to come to an end

And it finally does
And she is filled with regret
Still not justly conscious
Of the course of her life she has just set

WHO AM I

At the lowest point of my life
I allowed my body to be a tool
By this man and that man
I allowed myself to be so used

It was just something that I did
One senseless act behind the other
One would hurt my feelings
And I'd console myself with another

I was in search of something
I think it was acceptance
Tearing away a little piece of me
With each corrupt experience

I stood in the mirror one day
And watched the image staring back at me
I was so young and naive
Living a life that left me so empty

I saw a young lady
Who was going the wrong way in life
Doing the unnecessary
Trying to make her wrongs feel right

But I was so off track
And so lost in the way to go
Not quite ready to call on God yet
So little did I know

THAT FIRST TIME...(WHO KNEW)

That first time he pushed me should've been the initial sign
But I was so young; it didn't really register in my mind

That this would be just the start, the very first of many
Incidences where he would go far beyond verbally attacking me

It started as a push into the wall, then came the slap across the face
Still unwilling to admit I was now in a dangerous place

The slap across the face turned into a solid punch in the gut
He would always be sorry afterwards and tearfully tell me he just
loved me so much

I knew I had to get out before it got really bad
But whenever I would try to leave, he would become violently mad

I remember one time, he grabbed me by the neck and threw me
across the room
Just because I told him I really wasn't in the mood

Then there was the incident in the car when it was dark and it was cold
I tried to leave him then, and he tried to drive us off the road

I said whatever I had to say at that point just to get home
I told him I'd always be with him; but in my head, I was already gone

Sad to say, that wasn't the actual time I found the courage to leave
Not even after he beat me in front of my son as he looked on
helplessly

It was actually the time when he was angry enough to come to my
job
He put me in a choke hold and dragged me down the hall

People looking on; nothing did they do, not a word did they say
But that was it for me; that was the actual day

That I said enough was enough, that there would be no more
Of the constant beratings and beatings; I finally closed that door

Thank you, God

STUCK ON STUPID

I've done it, done it again
I've fallen in love with the most stupid man

But I knew it; I knew it from the start
I knew that fool was gonna break my heart

But it's like I couldn't help myself; I jumped in head first
Now I'm sitting here with tears in my eyes, looking stupid, feeling
stupid, ready to curse

This is just a repeat pattern, repeated from my past
Falling into a romance that I knew wasn't gonna last

I tried to let it go at one time, just let it be
But he said it was unacceptable and he would not let me

So I chose to hold on and let whatever happen happen
Now my heart is involved and it's already been broken

I feel him pulling away, bit by bit
And I know it's someone else, I know it's another chic

And all he has to do is just tell me so
He's so stupid; just let me know

Give me that option of whether I want to be the other woman
Instead of trying to play head games, making me his dummy

I wanna tell him I know, tell him how I feel
Instead of pretending these feeling aren't even real

But when I talk to him, I just foolishly hold the phone
Thinking to myself—this just stupid and its wrong

Another heart break is not something I wanna go through
I wanna let him go, but I love him and wanna keep him too

Trying to hang on I know is just not smart
This man is going to rip my soul apart

What I need to do is just tell him exactly what's on my mind
Let him know I ain't *that* stupid and kick his butt out my life all at
the same time

PLEASE DON'T LEAVE

How could you do this to me
After all that we've been through
How could you leave and just let it be
Why are you doing this; what did I do

Tell me and I will make it right
We can put things back together
I promise, no more fights
I will make everything better

Just please, give us another chance
I love you, and you love me I know
Let me try to get back our romance
We just can't let this go

So, please, baby, don't leave
We can work this thing out
You mean everything to me
I'm suffocating; and it is you that I can't live without

I'M TOO THROUGH

Lord, Lord—I know you don't wanna here this
But I ain't got nobody else to listen

My brother said I could no longer talk to him about this man
But it's just because he don't know; he don't understand

I know my brother loves me and is just tired of seeing me this way
Angry, hurting, losing my mind and in such disarray

Anyway, Lord, the man don' lied again, playing with my mind
But I'm serious now; this the last doggone time

I'm not gon' keep taking this from him; I deserve better
I'm leaving; I ain't coming back no more—not again, not never

I know everybody has heard this thing so many times before
But this time I'm for sure; I ain't doing this thing no more

Always having some kind of excuse
To do just whatever in the heck it is he wants to doggone do

After the dust settles his butt comes begging me back
And I usually go, but not this time—nah; forget that

This was it; the last doggone time
I'm serious now—I ain't lyin'

HELP ME LORD

Okay, God; here I am again
Please help me break free from this selfish, crazy man

I know you've heard me say no, never no more
And I don't even wanna talk about it; this issue has become so
sore

I'm tired, exhausted—physically and mentally
My God, the power I gave this man over me

Lord, in your strength and not my own
I need you now; I realize I can't do this thing alone

Help me, Lord

SAME OLD SIN...

Father God, here I am again
I've fallen back into that same old sin
That keeps me from you and in this desperate place
I need you, Lord; I seek your face
I've made so many promises to you before
That I feel you don't want to hear them anymore
But I've allowed him back into my life
With a promise to me that I would be his wife
Broken promises, broken promises
But this time I thought it would be different

But yet, Lord, here I am again
Disgraced and back in this same old sin
I heard your warning in the midst of, felt you speak on the inside
of me
Once I let him back in my life, there was this unrest, a stripping of
my peace
Now my spiritual life is in such disarray
I need you in such a powerful way
I haven't been in my bible, fasting or praying
Again this wayward person, steadily straying
Back to who I used to be
Selfish, malicious and full of self pity

I have allowed us to disconnect
For a man you said no to, I showed you no respect
For that, I'm sorry; forgive my disrespect
Your instruction and word, I will no longer neglect
You are my God, not this man

And for my contempt, I will accept my reprimand
So here I am again, begging for your mercy
Asking for your grace and your love to shower over me

Once I'm back in your arms, I'll try hard never to stray again
It's just not worth it, especially for that same old sin
Lord, you are my everything; allow me to come back home
Embrace me in your arms; with you is where I belong

I love you, Lord.
Thank you for the gift of repentance.

I MADE HIM MY GOD

I want to reach deep within me and share a painful story
The story of the man who I allowed to tear away such a large part
of me

A replacement man was all he was initially meant to be
You know, the dude that I would call after a breakup to comfort
me

He was married and had a woman; I wasn't trying to dig too deep
into that
Dismissing his wife and any other of his baggage as any real fact

Somewhere along the line, I allowed him to become too close
Eventually no longer with his wife or his woman; I felt it was me
that he chose

He became my everything; everything that mattered
I felt like I would literally suffocate without him

Over time, I became agonizingly aware that he was just
indescribably bad for me
Everything about this man and his ways just made me crazy

Making me a person I didn't know anymore, becoming reckless
and destructive
Inconceivably irrational, obsessive, dangerously compulsive

We had this on/off thing; I ultimately knew we would always get
back together
Because in my mind and my heart, it was always and forever

For years, I allowed this constant manipulation, jerking me in and
out of his life
With promises of eventually ending his turmoil and making me
his wife

More than often I would leave, then he would beg me back
He knew I'd be mad for a while, but I'd get okay—he always knew
that

Plus, with that promise of marriage lingering overhead—that was
my motivation
But I was never quite prepared for the explosive devastation

He began playing head games, even worse than before
He was ripping me from the inside out, down to the core

He knew the hurt he was causing; he knew he was making me
insane
The more hurt I felt, the more tears he saw, he seemingly would
inflict even more pain

Until it became so explosive that I did the ultimate to get this man
out of my life
To pull myself away from all of this mental anguish and emotional
strife

He had pretty much turned his back on me anyway
And my gut was telling me that he had taken up with another lady

I turned to God in the midst of my angst, feeling lost and
confused
I felt ashamed of myself, I felt betrayed and unbelievably used

Over time I started to feel the peace of God in my life—finally
Which is why I felt utterly humiliated and defeated when I let him
manipulate himself back to me

My world again in turmoil, my peace now gone
In the midst of the chaos, I barely heard the voice of the Lord
telling me to just hold on

To Him and all that He had done for me
All that He will continue to do to restore my peace

I eventually found the strength to allow things to end, just to cease
And turned back to God and let him continue to heal me

Thank you, Lord

FATHER, FORGIVE ME

Father, forgive me for what I am about to do
I'm not trying to say I don't trust you

I'm just in the most dreadful place I've ever been
Lord, please forgive me of this terrible sin

I've just put myself in such a bad situation
And, God, I'm scared; it's gotten so complicated

I don't know how else to handle this
I just don't know what else to do to fix it

I've gotten pregnant with his baby
And now he has completely turned away from me

Apparently, he has taken up with another
And, Lord, it kills me to think that he may love her

If I don't do this, I will always be tied to this situation
I will be living in absolute chaotic frustration

And, Father God, I will never be able to let him go
And he'll never be with me like I want… I know

So, I'm doing this for my remaining sanity
This way he won't have something to always control me

Forgive me, Lord; this isn't the way I really want it to be
It's just the only way I know for me to be free

KAELYNN NICOLE

Your name would've been Kaelynn Nicole
This April you would've been four years old
A beautiful baby girl I will never know
A beautiful young lady I will never see grow

All because of my own selfish fears
I thought it was the right choice, but I wasn't thinking clear
I never got to whisper mommy loves you in your ear
I still get angry sometimes because I want you here

But I couldn't see past the situation that was in front of me
I had no faith in what God could make it be
I was scared, trying so desperately to break free
And for that, Baby Kaelynn, I'm so sorry

If only I had trusted God to bring me through
Right now I would be watching you
Being silly and playing around the way most kids do
Instead of regretting what I have to now accept as true

FEAR BOUND

For as long as I can remember, I've been bound by the spirit of fear
The effects this spirit has had on my life have been so amazingly severe

Torturous, incomprehensibly paralyzing, robbing me of a life of normalcy
Mentally lost and confused, emotionally void of hope is the struggle on the inside of me

Feeling self-conscious, anxious and paranoid all the time
Because of the lies Satan tells me that I hold on to in my mind

Held within my soul, held within my life
This is the battle of the flesh and the spirit that causes me so much strife

Lord, help me pull away from this place that I'm in
Lord, help me take back my life so that it may begin

2 Timothy 1:7 For God hath not given us the spirit of fear; but of power, and of love, and of a sound mind.

WHEN I FIRST REALIZED I HAD ANXIETY

I remember the first time I recognized I had anxiety
I was in the post office—my son and me
I was next in line; the line behind me was so long
So many people; wishing it would quickly move along
I was standing there with all kind of crazy thoughts going through
my mind
This place is too crowded, it's getting warm, etc.—and my 5 y/o
bursts out crying
My heart starts fluttering, chest becomes full, a rise in my throat
Everybody's looking at us—oh, Lord, what's wrong with this boy
I'm suddenly hot, sweat abruptly dripping from my face
My son's tugging on my shirt, pointing at his untied shoelace
All I could feel were all eyes on me
Thinking people judging what type mother I must be
I reluctantly bent down and tied my son's shoe
I felt faint; Lord, please don't let me fall out and look like a fool
I actually couldn't even remember the rest
Me and my son were in the truck is what I remember next
That's when I first realized I must have anxiety
As I had similar episodes before, but none so overwhelming

PANIC ATTACK

It starts as a rising lump in my throat
Feeling as though I'm about to choke
Then comes the fullness in my chest
Meeting the lump in the my throat, I become immediately
distressed
I'm irritable and growing increasingly angry
It's hot, so hot—just comes on suddenly
An exasperating tingling in my arms
Both hands start to go numb
Jittery, shaking terribly on the inside
Thoughts racing, from this to that, muddling my mind
They're going a mile a minute
Talking fast, rambling on, not finishing my sentences
All worked up, gotta do something, gotta move around
Frantic internally, need my Ativan, gotta calm down

Isaiah 41:13 For I the Lord thy God will hold thy right hand,
saying unto thee, Fear not; I will help thee

TO LIVE OUT LOUD

I was watching this movie on TV
And in the end, everyone was so happy
And I thought to myself; God, why not me
What's it really like to be that free

Laughing, dancing, just living out loud
With not a care in the word; free not bound
Not paranoid, looking over my shoulder, glancing around
Just free, not bound, living out loud

It must be nice, and I'm gonna experience it one day
To live out loud and not worry about what other people say
Not worried about how my expressions are conveyed
I'm just going to live out loud; for this I pray

Bless you, Lord

MY SPIRITUAL BEAST

It's my stronghold, my spiritual beast
Attacks me in my mind, and I have yet to experience my release

Comes like a flood, with so much aggression
To hard for me to fight; it's called depression

It consumes me until I'm emotionally drained
Negated of any happiness, only sadness remains

I can't stand it, hating this place I'm at
But too weak, too drained to try to fight back

I shut down, completely isolate myself
From all that love me, refusing any help

This place is home; this is where I dwell
I may not like it, but this is where I live

...LETTING THE ENEMY

Racing thoughts
Panic attacks
Mind unclear
...letting the enemy fill me with fear

Bound
Unable to pray
Unable to fast
...letting the enemy lock me in my past

Insane
Can't function
Can't cope
...letting the enemy strip me of any hope

Keeping me from being all God has called me to be
...letting the enemy have power over me

CLUBBING AND PARTYING WITH SATAN

It was a relationship that I understood, one that was easy
Which made it simple for Satan to get in my mind and manipulate me
Drawing me to the wrong things and places, that were corrupting
Making me act out in a way I wouldn't normally

There was a time, I wouldn't step foot in a club, a party-like situation
I was too shy, that would have been too complicated
Then I hung out with my girls and through their gentle manipulations
I found myself enjoying my first club night; I thought it was amazing

Of course, I couldn't enjoy it all on my own
That's where Satan came in and pulled me along
Drawing me into all things wrong
And before I knew it, I was drunk, and dancing to every song

I got introduced to this vodka called Absolute
Also another called Gray Goose
Oh, and don't forget the cranberry juice
Had me acting and feeling completely loose

Out on the dance floor, I felt completely free
With a drink in each hand, I was somebody else besides me
Out there dancing all nasty
And just being absolutely silly

This was new for me, and I liked the experience
I wanted to experience it every weekend
Drinking and clubbing soon became my thing
Me and my girls would get dressed and go to whatever local club
scene

Then came the men, that were all in my face
All usually wanting to take me to their place
Initially, I'd say no; they weren't my taste
But there was occasionally that guy that I would enjoy the chase

Eventually, I started a new prayer life, and my perspective
changed
The fun in it no longer remained
There was something about me that wasn't the same
My perceptions had sharpened and started to change

I got to the point where I would go, but would feel out of place
Not drinking or dancing; instead talking with God about my mind
state
Telling him how I wish I wasn't there, and at home I should've
stayed
With my son, who didn't want me to go out anyway

Yes, it had gotten to the point, where my son would feel neglected
Because each weekend, instead of him, it was the clubs and the
men I selected
Instead of being home with my beautiful boy making him feel
protected
Coming into my parents home all times of night, making them
feel disrespected

All *"good"* things have to come to an end
No more time in bars and clubs I would spend
That had me blinded for a while, but I soon started to comprehend
Because of my prayer to God, my inner change had began

That part of my relationship with Satan was over officially
In that area, he had no more control over me
Not to have me drunk in clubs, sleeping around with men, or such things
I had a new outlook, and it was God Almighty

Thank you, Jesus

MY FEAR OF REJECTION

There is an issue closely related to my anxiety and depression
That I struggle desperately with; it's my fear of rejection

The irrational fear of nonacceptance of everything about me
Leaving me overdependent in affirmations, struggling with self identity

Where I leave my self-satisfaction and self beliefs in the hands of someone else
Struggling with low self-esteem and inability to have confidence in myself

It has negatively affected every important relationship in my life
Leaving me saddened and lonely, feeling contrite

Father God, help Me

TO BE FREE

What's it like to be free
Unrestricted, without boundary
Lord Jesus, please free me

I watch other people so carefree
But I'm bound, locked up mentally
Please, Almighty God, free me

I'm tired of living a façade; fake and phony
The persona of being happy
God Most High, please free me

I just want to live
Unrestrained, not imprisoned, but at liberty
Lord of Peace, PLEASE
Set me free

THE REVELATION OF ME

It was truly a harsh reality
When I asked God to reveal me to me

Anger, bitterness, malice—all places so dark
Selfishness, unforgiveness, pride—all held up in my heart

In all this muddled negativity, I slowly drown
Desperately wanting this self-built wall to come down

Because in this place, I feel so stuck
Tired, so tired, just ready to give up

I've cried out to God, but sometimes I feel He won't hear me
Which makes it easier for me to settle in my own self pity

But it was upon my request that he showed me who I've been
Now it's up to me, with His help, to move away from this internal sin

LOOKING FOR A RELEASE

The lies I've told have had such a great impact
Of such an immense magnitude and I can't take them back
And in the midst of, I'm under so much attack

They've altered the course of my life
My untamed tongue has me living in strife
And the feelings on the inside of me are so contrite

I need a cleansing of the soul; a release of my transgressions
A liberation of my discretions
I turn to you, Lord, and make my confessions

DRAW IT OUT

Like fire shut up in my bones—that's how I would describe
This spiritual gift God has placed on the inside

An internal tugging, pulling on me every day
But when I try to speak it I've got nothing to say

A constant nagging thought in my head
I prepare to write it but stare at blank paper instead

Frustration often overtakes me
Finally telling God, "Draw it out or let me be!"

Immediately convicted by the words I've just said
I then go to the bible to get my spirit fed

"What Lord? What is it gonna take?"
I'm suddenly drawn to Psalms 138:8

I'm reminded that the Lord will fulfill his purpose for me
And that simple knowledge brings me an abrupt inner peace

It is in God I will trust

MY PRAYER

Heavenly Father, I'm calling out to you
My life is such a chaotic mess
I have been living in sin and doing wrong
I must confess

I have lied, cheated in life
And played emotionally targeted games
I have been an adulteress, Father
And have had little to no shame

Lord, I've learned
That this is not the way to be
I need you Father
To guide and protect me

My heart is corrupt
It's not in the right place
I need you, The Most High One
To step in and show me the right way

I need you, Lord
To make me strong where I am weak
I need you, Father God
To guide and protect me

I'm covered in sin's filth
I'm so unclean
Guide me into a spirituality
So that more of you and less of me is seen

Forgive my transgressions
And wash me clean in the blood of the lamb
  Lead me, oh Lord, into the presence
Of the great I AM

In Jesus' Name
Amen

THE SILENT TORTURER

Waking at night, tears in my eyes
Sweat dripping, silent cries

Close my eyes, close them tight
Thoughts of the enemy, I try to fight

But I can't; unwanted thoughts invade my head
Giving in to defeatism and meditating on his tortures instead

I'm feeling like I'm spinning out of control
Open my eyes, and the tears begin to flow

A minute passes and I wipe them all away
Then I fall to my knees and begin to pray

This enemy has had me defeated; he has come to destroy
He has stolen my mind, stripped me of my peace and all of my joy
Father, lift from me this anger and unforgiveness in my heart, this
anxiety and depression that has taken over my soul
Help me, Lord, to submissively give you all the control

In Jesus' Name
Amen

A LETTER TO DADDY

Hey Pop,

Just wanted to drop a line or two
First to say how much I really do love you
Also to thank you for always being the very best dad
Which makes watching you decline these days so unbelievably
sad
Pop, I love you with all of my heart
And it rips my soul to see you the way that you are
You hardly resemble the man that you were before
Every day, I see you struggle more and more
How can I stop you on this destructive road you're taking
And from making the bad choices you're now making
I've been watching this nearly five years now
Feeling helpless, praying to God to fix it somehow
Even though, I do take full blame for your strife
For reintroducing alcohol back into your life
Though unintentional, I feel I brought you back to this place
You even said so yourself; you said it to my face
Now I live with this immense internal guilt
You just don't know how terrible I feel
Leaving this with God is all I know to do
I pray that he'll heal and restore you

Love,

Your Baby Girl

MEMORIES...

I call unto you, Father
Loose me and set me free
So that I may be loosed in my mind
From all these binding memories

That keep me locked in this place
I no longer wish to be
Plagued, weighed down
Please, Father God, loose me

They creep up in my mind
When I'm not aware
They pull me back to this place
Overwhelmingly so much despair

I even avoid certain places
So as not to have to be confronted
With a past that emotionally whipped me
And left me tormented

So, Lord, loose me
So that I may let it go
So that I will no longer live in a past
I no longer want to know

Praise be unto you, Lord

FAMILY FOLK AIN'T NO JOKE

Lord, Lord, Lord
I declare
I'm all over the place
Emotionally all up in the air

I'm livid,
So exceedingly angry
With family folk
Screwing over me

I'm fuming,
Anxious and ready to snap
I'd feel a little bit better
If a few people I could just slap

But your word says
Vengeance is mine
And, Lord, that's good and all
But sometimes you take too much time

Lord, let me get'em
Make them pay
For the crap they pulled, the lies they told
To hurt me this way

I know I'm suppose to wait on you
But you're taking too long
And, God, hear me when I say
Right is right and wrong is wrong

STILL THE FAMILY

Lord, Jesus, deliver me from this family of mine
All this back-biting, sneakiness, dirtiness and lyin'

Lord, my Lord, I ain't never seen nothing like this
And I know everybody's family has a little bit of foolishness

But, Father, I think mine is just on a whole 'nother level
They just act like a bunch of spiteful little devils

And it's pissing me off, putting me in the middle
Because some of the stuff they fight over is so trifling and little

They sit around one day and talk behind each other's back
The next day they grinning like ain't nothing—just like that

Father, God, I just don't understand
How they do their dirt, then hide their hand

It really just don't make no sense
Lord, dear Lord, I'm so darn sick of it

AUNTIE

I stood over her hospital bed and watched intensely
My aunt's time was winding down; she was about to leave this
earth
And I thought to myself
What was her life really worth

She never seemed happy, was mean-spirited and vindictive
Spiteful, bitter, with such an angry disposition
But who I was to judge
I never knew much about her position

I was told she was like that even as a child
So I never knew where all the anger and bitterness really started
I never really knew just when, how and what
Corrupted her heart

Then maybe it wasn't corrupted
Maybe it was just broken
From whatever, whenever
Maybe she felt unloved and lonely

What I know is
She always treated me unfavorably
Even as a child
Never understood why she didn't seem to like me

She was so negative, always said such ugly things
As an adult when I married
She told people
I must be pregnant

Mean and hateful and would often speak as such
As far as I can tell without regret
She suffered miserably inside and out
Yet, no remorse did I ever see her express

In her very last days
I started to see her differently
I didn't see her as I had growing up
Evil and malicious—monstrously

When I looked down at her
I saw this broken spirit
Who needed and sought love
But never actually received it

I would probably say
She got as good as she gave
And even as an adult
I never understood how she would habitually behave

So in the end
Was it a situation where you reap what you sow
The love she gave here on earth
Was returned to her as such tenfold

As she took her last breath
Everyone started to hoop and holler
Was it an outpour of love
Or guilt that now follows

Because, as far as I could see she wasn't loved
The way a mother, aunt or sister should've been

But she never gave it either
Not that I could see to any full extent

But what went on inside of her in the last moments
Who knew
Who really knew in the end
How much her spirit actually grew

It is my hope and belief
That she made peace with God
That her spirit was received
And finally receives the love I feel she so longingly sought

SEARCH MY HEART

There are secrets of my heart that are unknown to me
There's a tugging on the inside; Lord, search me

Search my heart and reveal to me what's there
On the inside that has me so conflicted and despaired

Search my heart, Almighty God, and remove my iniquities
That keeps me from you, as there are many

I love you, Lord, and my greatest desire is to be close to you
So search me, God; shall any impurities of my heart be removed

HUMBLED...

Okay, God, I've tried it my way and I've failed miserably
I'm on the brink of losing my mind; I mean really
I come to you as humble as I know how
I'm laying flat with my face to the ground
Lord, I need you more than anything
I've really seemed to have made a mess of things
My heart is broken and my life is a mess
Lord, I've failed terribly if this was a test
All I want now is to rest in you
I'm weary and I'm tired and don't know what else to do
Lord, your word says you will give rest to the weary
And right now, Father, that is me
Break me, Lord; have your way
I submit myself to you this here day
So that your will be done and not my own
Help me to let go of self because I know it's wrong
Help me to keep my mind stayed on you
In all things, keep me in the spirit as I hold on to what's true

In Jesus' Name
Amen

S.O.S.

Angst causing frustration
And increasing lack of motivation
All this aggravation
There is restoration...

Bound and unfree
It's all tied up in anxiety
Or locked inside a memory
I will give you peace...

Screaming on the inside, can't get out
Double-minded, confused, filled with doubt
The chaos in my head is so incredibly loud
Stillness of your mind will be brought about...

Emotionally battered
Broken and tattered
Faith now shattered
I am all that truly matters...

I'm tired, Lord
You are my Lord and Savior
Save me from myself
I've just been waiting for you to ask for my help...

THE "CHURCH EXPERIENCE"

I woke this morning feeling very heavy
Immediately, I told Satan to let go of me
It was Sunday morning and I was going to church
Even though I didn't desire to go very much
I made myself get up, and soon thereafter
Confessing to God my mind-set while in the shower

Eventually, I entered the tattered, old church building
Lord, what is this heaviness that I'm feeling
It was uneasy, almost angry; the spirit is quenched
I didn't want to be there to any extent
I looked around the parishioners and finally found a seat
Once again telling Satan to let go of me
I'm determined to have the full "church experience"
But instead feeling nothing but complete annoyance

The word is preached, and the spirit is on the move
All around me, people are shouting praises of hallelujah
I sit quietly, totally unmoved by the Holy Spirit
The hold the devil has on me is so implicit
Church is over, and it's time for alter call
I don't move, I don't budge at all
So much for that determined "church experience"
Satan took full control of it
I left church exactly like I came
Angry, uneasy; Lord, I was ashamed

ALTER CALL

Standing at the alter, face filled with tears
Not crying because of the spirit, but frustrated because I can't hear

Brother Wilson's trying to pray, and Sister May has broke out into song
And I know she's in worship and all, but she's off key and that's just wrong

Deciding that I'll concentrate on my own personal prayers
Laying all my stuff out there for God to just leave it there

Then there's a piercing noise in my ear; Sister Eloise begins to shout
And it was funny because not ten minutes ago, she was cussing a deacon out

Sister Odessa as usual, her spirit has become slain
And it's always hard for the person next to her because she has a two hundred-fifty pound frame

She starts to lean back and slowly begins to fall
Brother Tom is a small man, I bet he wished he'd sat out alter call

So now it's all over, and everyone takes their seat
Can't wait to see what happens on alter call next week

THE HOLE IN MY PURSE

It's that time of month again
To sit down with my check book and pen

Time to figure out the bills that can wait and those to pay now
At what point did it get this bad… and how

Probably when I started rationalizing with God why I couldn't
pay my tithes
Now every bill in my house is at least two months behind

I used to make my tithes the first thing on my monthly list
Eventually finding its way to the bottom and ultimately no longer
exists

Now it seems like the money that is made goes absolutely
nowhere
Gone before its gotten; almost like it was never there

There appears to be a hole in my purse
That seemingly got there when I stopped putting God first

Haggai 1:6 Ye have sown much, and bring in little; ye eat, but ye
have not enough; ye drink, but ye are not filled with drink; ye
clothe you, but there is none warm; and he that earneth wages
earneth wages to put it into a bag with holes.

MY TITHES...

Another Sunday morning and I'm getting ready to go to church
Got my tithes ready; got it in my purse

It's one hundred dollars and I intend to pay
I made up in my mind I wasn't going to rob God today

Service is over and the stewards are standing up front with the collection plates
I pull out my little brown envelope and begin to debate

If I pay my tithes, I can't buy the groceries we need
If I can't buy food, then what will we eat

If I pay my tithes, that'll take all my little money
If that happens, what about unexpected emergencies

I only get paid twice a month, what will I do
And, Lord, I know this sounds like I don't trust you

I clutch the envelope in my hand, trying to lay all my worries aside
Telling the devil to get out of my head and stop playing with my mind

I walk to the front and lay my tithes on the table telling God it's a start
My seed of faith and learning to trust you with all my heart

It is in you, Lord, that I trust....

I'M CALLING ON YOU

Okay, God, I'm just not having a good day
Probably because I got up this morning and didn't pray
I didn't take time to properly acknowledge you
And give you thanks for all the things that you do
Now this entire day has gone completely wrong
And to be honest, I've felt the urge to pray all day long
But I wouldn't, I couldn't get down on my knees
Even though to call on you is what I know I needed
Now I'm sitting here with tears in my eyes
So bothered, Lord, and I truthfully know why
I've been sitting here all day meditating on the wrong things
And I've allowed the enemy to come in so it seems
And he has me under so much attack
And either I'm too tired or too lazy to try to fight back
Forgive me, Father, because I didn't obey
When I know that you told me to get on my knees and pray
So here I am; I'm calling on you now
To pull me from this attack that I've seemingly allowed

AAAGGHH!!!

God, in this moment I'm so angry with you
Look at all the hell that I'm going through

My entire life is an absolute mess
Look at this; you call this blessed

By all these problems, I'm surrounded
Where are you; you're nowhere around me

I pray and I pray, and things get worse
What is this, Lord; some kind of a curse

Because that's exactly how it feels
Is this what being in Christ really is

Problem after problem, struggle behind struggle
Is dwelling in you always such a tussle

What about that abundant life; I don't understand
This place I'm in; is it part of your plan

Because if it is, Lord, I just don't know
It's too much for me, tugging at me so

Romans 8:28 And we know that all things work together for good
to them that love God, to them who are the called according to
his purpose

WHERE ARE YOU, LORD

I've cried out to you, yet I'm still here
In this place of chaos, destruction and fear

All these feelings overtake me and in them I drown
Where are you, Lord; I don't feel you around

I'm calling on you, broken and in despair
But you turn a deaf ear and it doesn't seem fair

The harder I pray, the worse things seem to get
The more I stay on bended knee, the less my desires are met

I asked You to bless us financially, and I'm more and more in debt
My job is slowing and economically we're in such a mess

And then there is my dad; don't you hear my prayer
So why does it seem like the problem is getting bigger

I pray for a breakthrough in my depression and anxiety
I'm seemingly sadder and need more Ativan to calm me

My husband's been patient; though I feel he is weary
With all my woes; I fear that he'll leave me

So where are you Lord, when I need you so
Why do you not come when I need you the most

Beloved, I am here; I've been here all the time
In the midst of this chaos going on in your mind

You complain about money, yet you have a roof over your head
You have never gone hungry; have all your needs not been met

The situation with your dad, you gave it to me
Take your hands off and stop your constant worry

I know you are anxious and increasingly depressed
I am God Almighty, I can ease your distress

Your husband is strong; he's not going anywhere
He's a gift from me to you; I put him there

I've acknowledged your prayers; they have not gone unheard
There is an enemy out there that you have not yet conquered

Make up in your mind not to give in to this fallacious fate
Then and only then will you not be so discombobulated

I am your Lord, your God, and I will not forsake you
But you have to trust in me and believe that I am the truth

FROM ME TO YOU AND YOU TO ME

Dear Lord:

Forgive me my countless transgressions
That may have blocked many of my blessings
I've been bound by life's intimidations
Conflicted and confused with life's situations
I need to be moved from this low position
I need help with this difficult transition
My feet are planted in spoiled ground
Can't reach my release; You are nowhere to be found
Because You don't dwell in such a dark place
But I can't find the light; I can't see your face
I'm looking, searching; I don't see you, Lord
The height of the darkness seems to have soared
I'm calling, I'm screaming, but you don't hear me
Surely because I drown in my own iniquity

My Child:
I ask that foolish talk to cease
I am Lord, your God; I can give you peace
Stop dwelling in the darkness and seek harder the light
Then you will see my face if you seek with all of your might
You're calling, screaming; I do hear you
But so condemned by your sins, you don't believe this to be true
Humble yourself and confess your sins
I'll wash you in the blood of the lamb and you will be cleansed
I will anoint your head with oil and give you the anointing power

That is what you need and what you're calling for in this hour
Just bow down to me meek in prayer
I will ease all your conflict and relinquish your despair

WHEN I'M GOING THROUGH

Where are you, God, when I'm going through
The bigger question is when you're going through, where are you

**Are you on your knees; are you fasting and praying
Are you in the word, seeking and obeying**
I'm not always on me knees, and I don't always fast, but I do pray
I may be slightly disobedient, but I do read the word; just not every day

**Walking in obedience and following my instruction is a very huge part
Then, there is also the issue of the condition of your heart**

**What's in your heart, your mouth will speak
And I have to be honest, Beloved, with what I'm hearing, I have not been pleased**

**You want guidance and you seek direction, but yet you doubt
You straddle the fence, halfway in and halfway out**

Lord, my God, I'm trying my best to serve you
But there are so many days that I don't know what to do

**You are not giving me the best of you; you're double-minded
You're easily discouraged, walks in offense and not love, prideful and most often defiant**

**You walk in the way of the world and not in the spirit
But it is there for you; you just have to call upon it**

You have to rebuke the devil and all his evil ways
You have to dwell in me and let me have my way

Remember, my will be done, not your own
Yet you continue to walk in your own way because you fear
the unknown

Humble yourself, surrender your will to me
I will give you the peace that you so desperately seek

Thank you, Lord. I surrender myself to you
Your will be done in my life; show me what it is that you want me
to do

MY LITTLE TALK WITH GOD

I talked to God
And told Him that I'm troubled
I told him how I'm warring in my mind
And how every day is a struggle

I told Him how sad I can be
And how often times I get so depressed
Then I told Him how anxious I am
And how it usually makes me so stressed

I told him that I'm frequently mad
And how I get so angry
I then told Him how I harbor unforgiveness
And how it's tearing away at me

Finally, I told Him that I feel as though I'm spiralling out of
control
Then the Spirit told me to get on me knees
And humbly ask Him to save my soul

LORD, MY LORD

Have mercy dear Lord
Have mercy on me
I cry out to you Lord
Please have mercy

I'm so tired
Of this place that I'm in
Heavenly Father
I'm sick of this sin

My heart is anguished
So much despair
I cry out to you Lord
Cry out in prayer

Oh merciful Father
Save me from myself
I need you Lord…
Need your help

I've been here so long
It's all I know
It feels almost impossible
To let myself go

But I now know
All things are possible through Christ
So here I am Lord
I offer up to you my life

Rest, rule and reign
On the inside of me
Come dear Lord
Set me free

John 8:36 If the Son therefore shall make you free, ye shall be free
indeed.

SPEAK LORD

All these years bound by fear
Mind under attack
All these years the enemy has stolen from me
I now want them back

Years of malice
Self abuse, self defeated
Feeling broken down
Self hate, emotionally beaten

Years of tears
Streaming down my heart
Too low to get up
Could not set my self apart

Apart from the enemy
That had me so bound
Even though I knew where my release
And my strength could be found

A daily fight, a struggle
Within my own head
Even though I knew where to go
To get my mind and spirit fed

Part of me embraced
The place I was at
It was familiar—being depressed, lonely
Self loathing, sometimes wanting to be just that

God's tugging, pulling
Trying to bring me out
To that longed for place
Of love and peace I have no doubt

But so broken, defeated and low am I
I choose to stay
Fighting God tooth and nail
Every step of the way

At the same time calling out *Lord, Lord, please help me, please*
Ready to surrender so I drop to my knees

Knees bent, face to the ground
I start to confess to God
Where I'm bound

Tears flowing, loud sobbing
Lord speak to me, I'm tired of sitting idle
Lift up my eyes, look to the left
and there is my bible

God speaks and says
Everything you're searching for is found
Right there in that book
If you would just embrace me
like you used to and take a look

I grabbed my bible
Lord, just lead me where you want me to go
I let out a loud cry
Lord tell me what you want me to know

My child, if you would just open up your mind and heart
Listen to and spend some time with me
This bondage that you're in
You shall surely be set free

I randomly opened up my bible
My face tear streaked
The pages fell on Ephesians 6:10
And the Lord began to speak

Bless you, God

SAVED BUT NOT FREE

What does it mean to be saved
But not free
Does it mean I've let go of sin
But it hasn't let go of me

Is it going to church every Sunday
Sitting on the first pew
With my mind wandering here and there
Hollering my amens and hallelujahs all on cue

Is it having the appearance of a halo overhead
Seemingly having it all together
But internally still struggling, twisted, and tangled
And not really feeling entirely better

Feeling a bit confused
Because I feel I'm giving God my all
Secretly still drowning inside
Every Sunday being first to run to the front for alter call

Standing at the alter, face filled with tears
Completely mystified
Because I'm still harboring feelings of
Unforgiveness, anger, bitterness, and pride

Because as a Christian I'm doing
All I know to be done
But still feel bound by these feelings
That often creep on

I spend daily time with the Lord,
Read my bible, fast and pray
But still there is that old mind-set
That keeps getting in the way

How can I be a Christian
And still feel like this
Once I gave my life to Christ
Shouldn't there just be an earthly bliss

Now that I'm living a Christian life I shouldn't still feel set apart
I shouldn't still be harboring
All these ungodly feelings in my heart

I cry out, "Lord I've surrendered myself to you
Soul, mind and body
So why are these feelings I felt before
Still on the inside of me?"

All these years you've been not just in sin
But you've been sinned against
You're still oppressed
From all those past experiences

You're breaking the hold
The devil has on you
But you've got to break the one
You have on him too

Just like Lazarus being raised and loosed
So that he could be free
You've got to be loosed in your mind
And claim your victory

Look at where you're going
Instead of where you've been
Celebrate who you are now
Instead of who you were then

It doesn't happen overnight
But over time
You'll be transformed
Only by the daily renewal of your mind (Romans 12:2)

LORD, WHAT IS IT THAT YOU WANT ME TO SAY

Sometimes I get this urge to suddenly get down on my knees and pray
But I don't move; I rationalize with God because I don't know what it is that I'm to say
I know that the Lord wants me to get on my knees; I've felt this many times before
But I don't because I don't know what it is that I should pray for
I soon learned that when I don't know what to pray
To just fall on my knees in obedience anyway
I utter the words "Lord, have mercy" over and over again
And I wait for that feeling of peace just for being obedient

Romans 8:26 In the same way, the Spirit helps us in our weakness. We do not know what we ought to pray for, but the Spirit himself intercedes for us with groans that words cannot express.

THANK YOU

A lot of time has passed, and this is long overdue
But I have to take a moment just to say thank you

Thank you for the torturous hell that you brought into my life
Thank you for not following through and making me your wife

Thank you for all the misleading and broken promises
Thank you for pulling away from me and becoming so distant

Thank you for leaving me emotionally broken, confused and
tattered
Thank you for walking away at a most crucial point, leaving me
shattered

I have to take this moment and say thank you
Because if not for you, I would never have had to fight
For my mind, my spirit; I would have never called on Jesus the
Christ

Because that's when we call on Him, when we're so broken and
don't know what to do
So with all my heart, man, I thank you

Because of you and all of the above
I was able to find my one true love

Jesus
He built me back up and showed me something new
While I was holding on to the past, clinging so desperately to you

He showed me what love really is
He showed me how love should really feel

Then he sent me my husband whom I absolutely adore
He showed me that I didn't have to hurt anymore

And that there is such a thing as a love that doesn't hurt
That there is such a thing as being able to trust

So, again, thank you for all you put me through
And even though, you never really apologized, I forgive you

Lord, thank you for the release

CLEANING MY CLOSET

I got up this morning with this urge to clean
The house wasn't dirty; I wasn't sure the meaning

I got up anyway and put on my mixed gospel CD
And said okay, Lord; go ahead; deal with me

I walked in the closet and stared at the clutter
I partially smiled and not a word did I utter

I knew what is was that God was trying to say
The closet represented my mind, and I was to start cleaning today

Though an enormous task and a chaotic mess
I reluctantly began the extended, tedious process

So much to deal with, so much to sort out
That filled my head with confusion and doubt

Stuff from the past that wasn't useful anymore
Stuff that I probably didn't even need before

Things just sitting there taking up space
Never wanting to throw it out; you know—just in case

But I had to rid myself of all useless things—it was time
Just like I had to clear up and clear out the muddle of my mind

I was tired and only halfway done, partially the way through
But I was determined to throw out the past and make room for all
things new

Thank you, Father

I APOLOGIZE

There have been so many wonderful people to come through my
life
That I usually let go of or push away for reasons that are not right
I have had some dedicated people who would later understand
Even after I waited months or years to call and make amends
But what can I say; every time I have an episode of depression
It's uncomfortable calling after so long and making that
confession
And then go into my rejection speech
Of how I was afraid to reach out because I no longer knew how
they felt about me
It was easier for me just to push people away when I was going
through
I was bitter and alone, but it's what I knew to do
I didn't want to bring anyone along into my depressed and
anxious world
Even though, I hated what I did, and I was such a lonely girl
So, nevertheless, this is long over do
But needs to be told to all of you
The way I am when I'm depressed; how without explanation I
push you away from me
Please, accept my deepest, heartfelt, sincerest apology

Much Love

THE LOVE OF A GOOD MAN

Something beautiful is the love of a good man
It used to be something beyond what I could comprehend

Because I had so many bad experiences
With a number of different acquaintances

And now this beautiful man has presented himself to me
Certainly a man given to me by God Almighty

Because I've never seen one so patient and kind
With a heart of gold, and he's all mine

He deals with every aspect of my personality
And he literally loves the hell out of me

He watches me go through my emotional difficulties
And when I tell you this man prays fervently for me

I mean he puts self aside and it's all about his wife
Me—the one who he pledged the rest of his life

And trust—that's something new, but I no longer worry
About where he's at, what he says he's doing—whatever he
tells me

And I'm so thankful for him, because there is none better
It is truly my belief the Almighty brought us together

And that all that hell I went through before
Was just to prepare me for my husband that much more

Because, had I not gone through everything I went through
I would never be able to appreciate someone as special as my
dude

So, thank you, Lord, for this precious gift
I promise to always love and treasure it

INNER PEACE (RESTING)

I always seemed to get myself in tight situations...
That strained my life, my heart and mind, and caused complications
I needed to take time and self heal before I would self destruct
I needed to find a path in my life that wouldn't hurt as much
I needed to find a road to joy and inner peace
Instead of traveling down the path of pain, anger, and grief
Soul searching, heart healing—that's what I would need
Peace of mind, a rested soul, I would need to find for me
The path that I found was the one back to Jesus the Christ
I gave myself back to Him to rule and reign in my life

Matthew 11:28 Come to me, all you who are weary and burdened, and I will give you rest.

I PRAY…

I pray a prayer of thankfulness
For all that He has done
How He has moved in my life exceedingly, abundantly and
beyond

I pray a prayer of forgiveness
Of my sins by word, thought or deed
To place forgiveness in my heart so that I may forgive others as
He has forgiven me

I pray a prayer of blessings
To rain down on me, my family and friends
To bless us all mightily and richly to no end

I pray a prayer for those less fortunate
Those unable or unwilling to pray for themselves
So that He will lift them tremendously, and in Him they will
propel

Thank you, Lord
These are all the things that's on my heart today
All these things in the mighty name of Jesus I pray

Amen

I BLESS YOUR NAME

When I think of where I've been
I think of how I'm blessed
I think of how you heard my cry
And put my soul at rest

I thank you Father
Simply for who you are
I look at where I was in life
And Lord you've brought me so far

I thank you for the trials
And the tribulations
That helped to shape and mold me
Coming out of those situations

If you never do another thing in my life
I can't and won't complain
Because you've done far and beyond
And I'll forever bless your name

HALLELUJAH TO YOUR NAME

I thank you, Dear Lord, for allowing me to see another day
I'm thankful for how you continue to bless me in your wondrous ways
Though undeserving, you continue to shower me with your merciful grace
I lift you up and bless your name and give you the highest praise
Hallelujah, hallelujah, hallelujah to your magnificent name

I'm praising you for the precious blood of your son
I'm praising you for all the phenomenal things in my life you have done
I give you praise for the darkness you've brought me from
And particularly for the victories in Christ that I have won
I praise you, God Almighty, for the strength you give me to continue on

I marvel in your astounding Holy Ghost power
That comforts me day in and day out, and right now in this hour
For you, Father, my spirit is now on fire
And when I praise your name, I feel so empowered
Hallelujah, hallelujah, hallelujah; I'll continue to lift you up higher and higher

BEFORE YOU SAY I DO

At an early age, we women tend to fantasize
About "how wonderful life would be
When that man I love so
Finally says I do to me"

A big beautiful house
At least two perfect kids
Sometimes we don't get the fantasy
Instead this thing called life happens

You'll go through some bad relationships
That will scar and emotionally break you
You'll make a couple of life altering choices
That will do a lot of emotional damage too

Yet, you continue to pray to God
To send you that special love
Before you have processed and dealt with
All of the stuff above

A man finally comes along
And you feel he's heaven sent
He professes his undying love
And says he is ready to commit

But before you rush anything
Before you say I do
There are a couple of things
I want to alert you to

If you rush into a marriage
Before you've dealt with all of your stuff
You'll become weighed down, overwhelmed
And it will become way too much

Because you didn't deal with your anger, bitterness
Selfishness and pride—all these things in you
Now you're trying to tackle it inside of a marriage
All of that plus coping with his feelings too

You didn't take the time you needed
To identify yourself in Christ
To let him heal and restore you
Now you're living in strife

So before you commit
And say those treasured words "I do"
Take a little "me time"
And let God deal with you

You can't say yes to someone else
Before you say yes to God
You'll be in this covenant relationship
Struggling, exhausted with living a façade

Marriage is not to be taken lightly
It is hard and it is exceptionally serious
Trust what I say
As I speak from a little bit of experience

LET GO AND LET GOD

We tend to block our own blessings
Holding on to things God has said no to
Missing out on all the newness
That He's trying to bring to you

He's trying to move us from the past
To get us to let go of precedent hurt and anger
He is trying to move us in a place
Where we are able to go out and minister

A hard lesson learned
Couldn't quite understand the place I was in
But I soon learned it was because I had yet to let go of stuff
God said no to in the beginning

I also had to learn that the hell I went through in life
Wasn't just for me
Through my growth, I had to allow myself to be so used by God
Allowing my hurt and pain to become my ministry

I had to get to a place in life
Where God felt he could trust me
To suffer the pain and go through the hell
Then go out and tell somebody

Look where God has brought me from
Look what God can do
Allow Him to heal your brokenness and use your pain
So that you may be a testimony too

LETTING GO

Let go when a situation strips your peace of mind
Stop asking God for some type of miraculous sign
They're there—stressed out, sleepless nights, burdens upon your heart
Situations weighing heavy and ripping your soul apart
Yet, you still fall on your knees looking towards the sky
Asking God the same already answered question—why, Lord, why
He has already answered in so many different ways
What exactly are you looking for God to now say
He has spoken already; you just didn't want to hear it
He's spoken it so many times, clearly, down into your spirit
And I know from experience to say "let it go" is easier said than done
But trust, it will only get worse the longer you hold on
You'll lose the parts of yourself that you haven't already lost
You'll develop a destructive pattern where your sanity may be the cost
Sometimes letting go is the only rational thing to do
What God has in store is truly the better choice for you

FOR THAT BEAUTIFUL MAN

You beautiful man with a heart of gold
You have a story that needs to be told
It's on your face; it's in your eyes
How you have been used, abused, demasculinized
You're kind and giving, and to others it makes you weak
But you're humble and gentle, and your spirit is so meek
I see it often; I see how people mistreat you
And it makes you want to turn cold and become just as cruel
But God has his hands on you, and you couldn't if you tried
Because it would tear you up and eat away on you on the inside

You beautiful man; continue to be just as beautiful as you are
Your light will shine as bright as a star
You'll one day have everything you desire
Because of God's magnificent anointing power
Find out who you are in Christ
Let him guide you through your life
He'll strengthen you where you're weak
While you continue to be just as meek
He'll remove those around you without your best interest at heart
From those, you will most definitely be set apart
And brought into the presence of the people of the Lord
No longer accepting less than you deserve

God bless you

WHAT HAPPENED TO THE CHURCH

When did the church become a place just for show
Where you come in filled with pride and sit on the front row

And put on the face that everything is unquestionably fine
When you're internally broken, struggling and losing your mind

The religious folk that come into the church pretending all is right
With this pretense of religion; falsely professing Christ

Those that stand arrogantly in judgment of others
Instead of humbling themselves and reaching out to another

They wear a scowl on their face, not the hint of a smile
Not one pleasantry is uttered from their mouth

The religious folk that make people feel they're in bad taste
Make them feel that they are inapt and in the wrong place

Aside from worship, the church is a spiritual place of healing
Where we can come in broken, in sin, and tell God what we're feeling

Have we forgotten church is a place we can bring our transgressions
Where we can stand at the alter of God and make our confessions

Allow him to wash us clean from sin's filth and leave him our issues
What happened to church; what has it come to

SISTER GIRL, SISTER GIRL

Sister Girl, Sister Girl, I see your struggle
You wear it on your face, your internal tussle
I know it too well; I've been there before
And I praise God to the highest degree that I ain't there no more
So let me reach out to you as I know what's going on
Through our conversations, I know you feel alone
You've struggled with this relationship and he has finally left you
You're grasping on to the wrong things that will only further break you

In the midst of your heartache, in the midst of your pain, God is there
I know it doesn't feel like it, because you're in so much despair
But you held on to that relationship as long as you could
You compromised yourself way more than you should
I know from experience that what you compromise yourself for, you will lose
You can't satisfy someone else more than you try to satisfy you
It's an endless, exhausting, hopeless task
Are the end results truly worth it; you really have to ask

I am a living testimony that there is life after the man
At one time, my mind didn't wrap around it; I couldn't understand
How could I go on without him, live beyond the moment
But God showed me in words that were unspoken
I allowed him to heal me; I reached out in faith
And it didn't happen all at once, but the hurt started to abate
The feelings of bitterness, resentment and malice all held up inside me

God is now allowing me to use it as part of my ministry

So Sister Girl, Sister Girl, just know that God has his hands on you
Know that you're not alone in all that you're going through
He knows your hurt and has seen your tears
He knows right now how broken beyond repair you feel
Don't spend too much time crying over rejected things
God has something better for you; just wait and see
You've just got to get out of your own way and let your blessings flow
Let God into your heart and life; just let go

GIRL, LET ME TALK TO YOU

Girl…Sometimes I just want to grab you and shake you
As I watch some of the things that you consciously do
A lot of things that you take yourself through
And in the end you become disgraced and used

Trust, I ain't trying to judge; cause these are some replays of mine
Things I allowed myself to go through once upon a time
Where I let a man manipulate me out of my mind
And the entire time he was just habitually lying

So, don't you see, I recognize what's going on
And, baby girl, the way he treats you is just wrong
You deserve better, and you've been waiting so long
But in the end, you're always left alone

I watch you put more of yourself into these things than you get out
And he truly is showing you what he's all about
I once told you, believe what they do and not what they spout
That way you will never really be in doubt

Because if he's saying he cares, but is never there
Got you dressed up, waiting, but never takes you anywhere
Not the first time, but we're talking multiple times here
His actions are showing you that he really doesn't care

And this is a repeat cycle that you just keep repeating
You just need to take some time for "God and me"
And for a while, just let these silly men be
As you find yourself through God's wondrous mysteries

Learn to love yourself, as you would like to be loved
Not just tolerated or occasionally thought of
But really loved, like that of above
Loved...God's type of love

YOU CAN'T SEE YOU

You can't see you
And all the things that you do
All the choices that you make
You have a tendency to blame others for your mistakes
You can't see you
Or perhaps you don't want to see what you take people through
Especially your kids; all that they have to endure
Because of the amount of trouble for yourself that you always accrue
Then there is the lifestyle that they're exposed
And one of your kids cries at the thought of coming home
Says she wishes she was dead than to be there
To hear a child speak that way for me is so rare
But you can't see you and your role in this
You've got to make some changes in your life for the sake of your
kids
If you can't do it for you, think about them
Get your life together; you've got to leave him

He's been a huge part of your downfall for years
And you see this and have been for a while now, through all of
your tears
You leave, but yet you come back
And your kids are looking at you with lack of respect
And even if you can't see you for you
You've at least got to see what your kids are going through
There are years of pinned up suppression
There is either going to be an eruption of emotion or set in depression
Which I see one erupting and the other depressed
But you can't see you; you've got to get out of this mess
People try to talk to you, but you won't hear anybody but yourself

You curse people out, justify what you do, but you never ask for help
For years, you've been on this merry-go-round
Self destruction, befriending the wrong people, talking too much
has kept you down

It's time to move from this place that you're in
It's time to get out of all your sin
It's time to tell the devil; and you need to yell
That you will no longer live in his hell
That you will no longer live the same
And that it is time for you to make a change
Not just for you but for your kids
So that life for them won't be so dim
Grab on to God, and never let go
Only then, by faith, will you start to spiritually grow
And make right decisions through the wisdom of The Almighty
And just let this life as you've always known it just be
No one said it will be easy; it's hard
But you can start by submitting yourself, your troubles, and your
family to God

SECRETS OF YOUR HEART

The secrets of your heart that go untold
That linger around and flood your soul
No longer able to conceal, they start to unfold
They become secrets you can no longer hold

Secrets of your heart you try to hide
But they're starting to come out; externalize
You're wearing it on your face, seen in your eyes
The secrets that initially started in your mind

They're the secrets the enemy has whispered to you
The lies to keep you broken that he has used
To block your blessings and keep you confused
Keeping you from your profound breakthrough

These are the secrets of your heart that keep you in tears
Keep you walking around in outrageous fear
Unable to adequately live so it appears
You should listen to the secrets that God whispers in your ear

God's secrets of the heart are part of His plan
Which may be hard for you to right now understand
You have to have that crazy faith and embrace his outstretched
hand
And trust in the great I AM

MY HEART BREAKS FOR YOU

You're only 15 years old, carrying the weight of the world on your shoulders
The situations you've been exposed to in life have made you appear much older

But, now you're at your breaking point, have taken all you can take; you're depressed
About to internally erupt because of all that you suppress

You don't have an adult you can talk to; you feel alone and keep it all inside
You're so tired, and to my understanding there's even talk of suicide

But, baby girl, you are loved; come…let me put my arms around you
Let's pray together; let's tell God what you're going through

Oh, sweetie how I hurt for you; but we've got to trust God to make it better
I know it seems like the world is falling in on you; but this is the attack of the devil

I remember how excited you were when you first accepted Christ
My biggest concern then was the right people surrounding your life

You were surrounded by so much chaos and confusion; you were way too young for that
With no guidance to help you; now it has made you suddenly react

I so hurt for you; come...let me wrap you in my arms
And remember that God is the most important part
And even though I hurt for you
I have the confidence and faith that He will bring you through

I love you, sweetie

LITTLE TIFFANY AND YOU

Little Tiffany is so pretty; she looks just like you
I watch how she tries to emulate everything that you do

She idolizes you; to her you're her hero
And she wants to be just like you when she grows

What're you teaching her; are you teaching her the things of God
Are you raising her up in the way that you ought

Because from what I see, she is barely a teenager and is growing too fast
And before you know it, little boys will try to get in her pants

By the way, which are a little to snug in the hips
And the shirts are just as tight, not too much different

I ain't trying to get in your business, but I feel like we're close enough to say what I got to say
This is me on the outside looking in, and you raising her the wrong way

The things she sees, the things she's exposed to—the fighting with your husband, the different men
She is going to grow up thinking that this is how it is

It's okay to be married and break vows
To have another dude on the side is wild

She think its okay for a man to treat her this way
And just like you, hope that it gets better one day

But these are not the things to be teaching your daughter
You should be teaching the way of Christ and nurturing her

She is so very impressionable at this age
You've got to make some changes in the way you behave

You've got to teach your daughter right from wrong
Before it's too late, and the damage is already done

But before you can instill these things in her to do
You've got to first instill them in you

You've got to change your ways and the things that you do
For the sake of your daughter, so that these things she won't have
to go through

I know you dabble in the Lord a little bit, but it's time to fully
surrender yourself
Bow down to Jesus, thank Him for his precious blood, and then
ask for his help

It's not an overnight change, but over time
It's gonna be hard because it is a battle of the mind

Your daughter is such a vital part
That should encourage your much needed change to start

Be Blessed

REJECTION

All my life, by school mates, by coworkers, by family, I have felt rejected

I felt unwanted, sometimes unloved, and often times unaccepted

It took me almost my entire life to realize that rejection wasn't always about me

It very well may have been God protecting the anointing he placed on me explicitly

It may have been because I was desiring the wrong things, to hang with the wrong crowd

I was protected through rejection to keep my mind stayed on God and keep me grounded

A hard lesson learned but one that can now be understood and sought

As in the bible it teaches about the living Stone; rejected by men but chosen by God

This is when I learned that God had an anointing on my life, had an assignment for me

He didn't want me backsliding and picking up evil speaking and hypocrisy

He protected me through rejection—keeping me from cliques and such

And I have to say that I love Him, because He loved me just that much

1 Peter 2:4 As you come to him, the living Stone—rejected by men but chosen by God and precious to Him.

WHERE IS YOUR PEACE?

The enemy uses patterns of destruction against you
Your level of maturity in Christ can be assessed by what you in
return do

What kind of atmosphere do you present
Chaos, anxiety, depression—the enemy's presence

Where is your peace

Does your peace dwell in your stuff
If you didn't have it, would you love God just as much

Do you quickly react to external stimuli
Are you that carnal Christian where Satan easily manipulates
your mind

There are two different types of peace
Peace of the world and peace of Christ—which one do you
receive

The peace of the world is carnal, atmospheric, embedded within
one's surroundings
The peace of Christ passes all understanding, will not be moved
in chaos, is steadfast and astounding

Where is your peace

If you have the peace of God in your life; you've got that crazy peace
Where your world can be tumbling down, but you still got a song in your heart and praise on your lips cause you know "God got me"

So, where is your peace
Is it with God Almighty
Or in external stimulatory

Where is your peace

2 Thessalnians 3:16 Now the Lord of Peace himself gives you peace always by all means

IS THIS YOU??

First one to stroll in the church and sit on the first pew
First one to shout, "Praise Him, Hallelujah"
First to became slain in the spirit and everyone with a fan hovers
over you

Are you the head of every church committee
Are you over every bake sale and church charity
Are you the first to donate the church money

These things are all good too
But have you taken time to evaluate you
Your motives in all that you do

Are you busying yourself for some sort of acceptance
Are you burying yourself in the things of God to gain reverence
Or are these things that you simply find pleasant

Because with all these things and more that you do
Does not mean that God has found favor in you
In fact, works without faith is dead; read Hebrews

In essence, I'm saying all this to say
That above all, God wants us in relationship; no better time to
start than today
To get in the word, have faith, draw nearer to Him and
continuously pray

Because God knows your heart and all that you do
What it's about, who you're trying to please, what you're trying
to prove
God knows if it is about Him, the people or you

So if you're doing all of the above
But still don't have the heart to serve
God is not pleased with your many works

Furthermore, if you're doing all of the above without fail
But still no relationship with God, true loved not unveiled
Your soul is still destined to hell

Think about it...
Is this you??

TO BE MATURE SONS/DAUGH-TERS OF GOD

Are you a mature son/daughter of God
Have you rid yourself of all things not of God
Have you prepared your entire being to be holy
Have you made up in your mind to live obediently
Have you rid yourself of all worldly desires
Have you allowed yourself to be purified
Have you put away all evil thinking, such as malice and deceit
Gossiping, hypocrisy and worst of all—envy
Have you learned to walk in love and not offence
Or are your continuously guarded, always on the defense
These are some of the things that you must do to become mature in Christ
Putting away things of old, and allowing him to spiritually guide your life

IT IS FINISHED

Right now, Lord, I'm in complete reverence of you
All that you've been in my life, and all that you continue to do
I just hope my works have significantly pleased you

There were days when I would sit here—and I just didn't know
Those are the days that you wanted me to rest and just let go
Because when you wanted me to work, the words would just flow

Without much thought, the words would just flow
From you to me, and in the midst of, I noticed a spiritual growth
So as you used me to bless others, you were also blessing me; this
I now know

So, thank you, Father, for the wonderful gift that you have placed
on the inside
That for so long, I was almost ashamed of and would often try to
hide
There are still some things that I wrestle with, but I thank you for
dealing with my pride

God, I love you above all and any
And I hope this book of poems is used to bless many
As I'm sure you intend for it to reach the hands of plenty

There were so many evenings I was in anguish
Because I wanted the poems you gave me to be so beautifully
polished
Now, Lord, with your help—IT IS FINISHED

Thank you, Father